CREPES
BLINIS &
PANCAKES

Consultant Editor:
Valerie Ferguson

LORENZ BOOKS

Contents

Introduction

Crêpes, pancakes and blinis all bring an element of fun to meal times. Whether served simply with a squeeze of lemon juice and a sprinkling of sugar or filled with a rich seafood mixture, they are always a special treat. As an added bonus, they are quick and easy to make from store-cupboard ingredients, filling enough for the heartiest appetite and can be very economical.

Pancakes – an all-embracing term – are thicker and more substantial than crêpes. They may be filled and rolled or served with a topping. Crêpes are thinner with a lacier texture. They are usually filled and rolled or folded. Blinis, which originated in Russia, include yeast in a batter based on both wheat and buckwheat flours. They are generally smaller and thicker than western pancakes.

The range of fillings and toppings is almost endless – cheese, vegetables, fish, seafood, chicken, ham and mushrooms make superb savoury pancakes and crêpes, while melt-in-the-mouth desserts can include chocolate, fruit, nuts, jam, honey and syrup. Serve them plain or with sauces.

So, don't wait for Shrove Tuesday to make crêpes, blinis and pancakes, enjoy them all year round with the family or with friends.

Ingredients

MAKING THE BATTER

Pancake batter is very easy to make and consists of a few basic ingredients.

Flour You can use plain (all-purpose) or self-raising (self-rising) white or wholemeal (whole-wheat) flour. Buckwheat flour may also be used combined with wheat flour.

Eggs Fresh free-range eggs have the best flavour. They may be added whole or separated and the whites whisked for additional lightness.

Liquid Milk is the most usual liquid. Those watching their intake of fats can use semi-skimmed. Single (light) cream or buttermilk add extra richness and both beer and soda water produce puffier pancakes.

Chocolate Sweet pancakes can be transformed by adding cocoa powder or melted chocolate to the batter.

FILLINGS & TOPPINGS

A wide range of fresh and store-cupboard ingredients may be used for fillings and toppings.

Dairy Products Cheese is a perfect partner. Creamy cheese, such as mascarpone, and crumbly cheese, such as feta, make luscious fillings on their own or with vegetables or fruit. Harder cheeses, such as Cheddar and Gruyère, and blue cheeses, like Roquefort, can be used to flavour sauces for fillings or toppings. Soured cream is a traditional topping for blinis. Yogurt, crème fraîche and whipped cream are delicious on sweet pancakes and crêpes.

Fish & Seafood Fresh and smoked fish, usually in a creamy or cheese sauce, make perfect fillings for crêpes and pancakes. Smoked salmon and soured cream, garnished with a sprig of dill, is a classic combination. Most kinds of seafood – prawns (shrimp), mussels, crab and lobster meat – work well. The traditional way to serve blinis is topped with soured cream and a little caviar.

Poultry Both chicken and turkey make tasty pancake fillings and this is a good way to use up a leftover roast. Finely chop or mince the meat.

Left: Flour and eggs are the basis of pancake batter.

Left: Add chopped pieces of sliced ham to a pancake for a delicious savoury treat.

Ham Generally speaking, most meats are too dense in texture for filling pancakes or crêpes, but ham is the exception. It also combines well with other ingredients, such as mushrooms, asparagus or cheese.

Vegetables Almost all vegetables make excellent fillings and toppings. Roasted vegetables, such as peppers, are a good choice. Spinach, often combined with a creamy cheese, is a classic filling for crêpes.

Onions, shallots or leeks add extra flavour to a vegetable mix, which might also include carrots, beans, courgettes (zucchini) and sweetcorn. Fine asparagus spears look elegant in crêpes and taste fabulous.

Herbs & Spices

Use herbs, such as parsley, chives and basil to flavour savoury fillings, and spices, such as cinnamon and nutmeg, for dessert crêpes and pancakes.

Right: Sprinkle a little grated nutmeg onto a pancake for a tasty late-night supper.

Mushrooms Sautéed wild mushrooms or a mixture of wild and cultivated mushrooms are especially flavoursome. Use mushrooms on their own or with other ingredients.

Fruit All kinds of berries are delectable in pancakes or crêpes. Uncooked or fried bananas are truly scrumptious. Sliced oranges or chopped pineapple are very refreshing.

Syrups Maple syrup is traditional, but others, such as cane or corn syrup, make luscious toppings for pancakes – with or without butter. Honey works well too.

Nuts Almonds, walnuts, pine nuts and pecan nuts add a tasty accent to fillings and toppings.

Alcohol Port, Cointreau, cognac and Grand Marnier all make delicious additions to fillings and sauces.

Techniques

Batters differ depending on the combination of ingredients used.

Making a Batter

Batters consist mainly of flour, eggs and liquid. For a very light result, the eggs can be separated and the whites whisked and folded in.

1 Sift the flour into a bowl along with other dry ingredients such as sugar, ground spices etc.

2 Make a well in the centre and put in the eggs or egg yolks and some of the liquid.

3 With a wooden spoon, beat together the eggs and liquid in the well just to mix them.

4 Gradually draw in some of the flour from the sides, stirring vigorously.

5 When the mixture is smooth, stir in the remaining liquid. Stir just until the ingredients are combined – the trick is not to overmix. Leave the mixture in the refrigerator for about 20 minutes before using.

6 If the recipe specifies, whisk egg whites to a soft peak and fold them into the batter (made with yolks). Do this just before using the batter.

Crêpe & Pancake Tips

• The batter should be the same consistency of whipping cream.
• The batter can be made by hand using a wooden spoon or in a blender or food processor. Leave to stand before using.
• Your first crêpe may well be unsuccessful because it will test the consistency of the batter and the temperature of the pan, both of which may need adjusting.
• Crêpes can be made ahead of time. Cool, then stack them, interleaved with greaseproof paper, and wrap in foil. They can be refrigerated for up to 3 days or frozen for 1 month.
• A crêpe pan has a flat base and straight sides; these give the crêpe a well-defined edge.

Making Crêpes

Thin, lacy crêpes are wonderfully versatile. They can be served very simply with just lemon juice and sugar, or turned into more elaborate savoury or sweet dishes.

Basic Crêpe Batter
Makes about 12

INGREDIENTS
175 g/6 oz/1½ cups plain (all-purpose) flour
10 ml/2 tsp caster (superfine) sugar (for sweet crêpes)
2 eggs
450 ml/¾ pint/scant 2 cups milk
about 25 g/1 oz/2 tbsp butter, melted

1 Make the batter and leave to stand for 20 minutes. Heat a 20 cm/8 in crêpe pan over a moderate heat. The pan is ready when a few drops of water sprinkled on the surface jump and sizzle immediately.

2 Grease the pan lightly with a little melted butter. Pour 3–4 tablespoons batter into the pan. Quickly tilt and rotate the pan so the batter spreads out to cover the base thinly and evenly; pour out any excess batter.

3 Cook for 30–45 seconds, or until the pancake is set and small holes have appeared. If the cooking seems to be taking too long, increase the heat slightly. Lift the edge of the pancake with a palette knife; the base of the pancake should be lightly brown.

4 Shake the pan vigorously back and forth to loosen the pancake completely, then turn or flip it over. Cook the other side for about 30 seconds. Serve or leave to cool.

5 To fill crêpes: For folded crêpes, spread 45–60 ml/3–4 tbsp of filling over each crêpe. Fold the crêpe in half, then in half again. For rolled crêpes, put 45–60 ml/3–4 tbsp of filling near to one edge of each crêpe and roll up tightly from that side.

6 For parcels, spoon 45–60 ml/ 3–4 tbsp of filling into the centre of each crêpe. Fold the two opposite sides over the filling, then fold over the other two. Turn the parcel over for serving. Filled pancakes are usually baked before serving, to reheat them.

Pancakes with Soured Cream & Salmon

Bite-size buckwheat pancakes with a luxurious creamy topping make superb canapés to serve with pre-dinner drinks.

Makes 25

INGREDIENTS
75 g/3 oz/⅔ cup buckwheat flour
10 ml/2 tsp caster (superfine) sugar
1 egg
120 ml/4 fl oz/½ cup milk
25 g/1 oz/2 tbsp butter or margarine, melted
2.5 ml/½ tsp cream of tartar
1.5 ml/¼ tsp bicarbonate of soda (baking soda)
15 ml/1 tbsp water

FOR THE TOPPING
225 g/8 oz salmon fillet, skinned
juice of 1 lime or lemon
60 ml/4 tbsp extra virgin olive oil
45 ml/3 tbsp chopped fresh dill
150 ml/¼ pint/⅔ cup soured cream
¼ avocado, peeled and diced
45 ml/3 tbsp chopped fresh chives (optional)
salt
fresh dill sprigs, to garnish

1 Slice the salmon as thinly as possible. Place the slices, in one layer, in a large non-metallic dish.

2 Combine the lime or lemon juice, olive oil, chopped dill and a pinch of salt. Pour the mixture over the salmon. Cover and chill for several hours.

3 For the pancakes, combine the buckwheat flour and sugar in a mixing bowl. Set aside. Beat together the egg, milk and butter or margarine. Gradually stir the egg mixture into the flour mixture. Stir in the cream of tartar, bicarbonate of soda and water. Cover the bowl and let the batter stand for 1 hour.

4 With a sharp knife, cut the marinated salmon in thin strips.

5 To cook the pancakes, heat a heavy, non-stick frying pan. Using a large spoon, drop the batter into the pan to make small pancakes about 5 cm/2 in in diameter. When bubbles appear on the surface, turn over.

6 Cook for 1–2 minutes, until the other side is golden brown. Transfer the pancakes to a plate and continue until all the batter is used.

7 To serve, place a teaspoon of soured cream on each pancake and top with the marinated salmon. Sprinkle with the diced avocado and chives, if using, and garnish with dill sprigs.

Bourbon Pancakes with Asparagus & Ham

For a very grown up brunch, add bourbon to the batter and dressing.

Serves 4

INGREDIENTS
50 g/2 oz/½ cup self-raising (self-rising) flour
2.5 ml/½ tsp mustard powder
1 egg, beaten
60 ml/4 tbsp milk
15 ml/1 tbsp bourbon
butter, for greasing
8 cooked asparagus spears
8 slices of Parma ham

FOR THE DRESSING
45 ml/3 tbsp olive oil
15 ml/1 tbsp bourbon
salt and ground black pepper

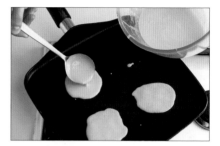

2 Heat a griddle or heavy-based frying pan. Grease it thoroughly. Drop spoonfuls of the batter on to the hot griddle to make four pancakes. (If you prefer, you can pour the batter into muffin rings placed on the griddle.) Cook for 2–3 minutes, until bubbles rise to the surface of each pancake and burst.

3 Turn the pancakes over with a palette knife and cook for 2–3 minutes more, until golden brown. Remove and keep hot while making four more pancakes in the same way.

1 Sift the flour and mustard powder into a bowl. Make a well in the centre and add the egg, milk and bourbon. Whisk the batter until smooth.

4 Mix the dressing ingredients together in a bowl. Taste and adjust the seasoning if necessary.

VARIATION: If you do not have bourbon you could use whisky.

5 Place two pancakes on each plate. Put an asparagus spear on top of each pancake, drape decoratively with a slice of Parma ham and spoon over a little of the dressing.

American Pancakes with Grilled Bacon

Serves 4

INGREDIENTS

175 g/6 oz/1½ cups plain (all-purpose) flour,
   sifted
15 ml/1 tbsp caster (superfine) sugar
2 large eggs
150 ml/¼ pint/⅔ cup milk
5 ml/1 tsp bicarbonate of soda (baking soda)
10 ml/2 tsp cream of tartar
vegetable oil, for frying
unsalted butter
maple syrup
crisply grilled (broiled) bacon
salt

1 To make the batter, mix together
the flour, sugar and a pinch of salt. In a
separate bowl, beat the eggs and milk
together, then gradually stir into the
flour, beating until smooth and thick.

2 Add the bicarbonate of soda and
cream of tartar, mix well, then cover
and chill until ready to cook.

3 Beat the batter again. Heat a little
oil in a heavy-based frying pan or
griddle. Drop spoonfuls of the mixture
into the pan, spaced well apart, and
cook over a fairly high heat until
bubbles appear on the surface of the
pancakes and the undersides become
golden brown.

4 Carefully turn the pancakes over
with a palette knife or fish slice and
cook briefly until golden underneath;
then transfer them to a heated serving
dish. Top each pancake with a little
butter and drizzle with maple syrup.
Serve with grilled bacon.

Matzo Pancakes with Spinach

Makes 10

INGREDIENTS
1 egg white
1 egg
120 ml/4 fl oz/½ cup water
40 g/1½ oz/⅓ cup fine-ground
   matzo meal
30–45 ml/2–3 tbsp vegetable oil

FOR THE TOPPING
225 g/8 oz fresh spinach
50 g/2 oz Cheddar cheese, grated
salt and ground black pepper

1 To make the topping, wash the spinach, drain and cook in a pan with no extra water for about 1 minute. Drain, press out the moisture and chop. Season well. Stir in half the cheese.

2 For the pancakes, whisk the egg white and egg until thick, then gradually add the water. Sprinkle in the matzo meal and beat until the mixture is smooth.

3 Heat a little oil in a small frying pan and drop in some of the mixture in large spoonfuls. Almost immediately turn them over and press the pancakes down slightly. Cook for another minute on the other side.

4 Repeat until the mixture is used up. Preheat the grill (broiler). Arrange the pancakes on a baking tray. Top each one with a little of the spinach mixture and sprinkle with the remaining cheese. Grill (broil) for 1–2 minutes and serve immediately.

Russian Buckwheat Blinis

This is a less expensive variation of one of Russia's most famous dishes – blinis with soured cream and caviar.

Serves 4

INGREDIENTS

75 g/3 oz/⅔ cup plain (all-purpose) flour
50 g/2 oz/½ cup buckwheat or
   wholemeal (whole-wheat) flour
2.5 ml/½ tsp salt
5 ml/1 tsp easy-blend (rapid-rise) dried yeast
175 ml/6 fl oz/¾ cup warm milk
25 g/1 oz/2 tbsp butter, melted
1 egg, separated
45 ml/3 tbsp vegetable oil

FOR THE TOPPINGS
150 ml/¼ pint/⅔ cup soured cream
30 ml/2 tbsp chopped fresh dill
50 g/2 oz/4 tbsp red or black
   lumpfish roe
115 g/4 oz smoked mackerel, skinned,
   boned and flaked
50 g/2 oz/4 tbsp unsalted butter, softened
finely grated rind of ½ lemon, plus shredded
   rind to garnish
lemon wedges, to serve

1 Sift the flours and salt into a large bowl, adding any bran left in the sieve. Stir in the yeast, then make a well in the centre. Pour in the milk and gradually beat in the flour until smooth. Cover with clear film (plastic wrap) and leave to rise for approximately 1 hour, or until the mixture has doubled in size.

2 Stir in the melted butter and egg yolk. Whisk the egg white in a bowl until stiff, and gently fold in. Cover and leave to stand for 20 minutes.

3 Heat 15 ml/1 tbsp of the oil in a large, heavy-based frying pan over a medium heat and drop in about four spoonfuls of batter. Cook for 1–2 minutes, or until bubbles appear on top.

4 Turn them over and cook for a further 1 minute, or until both sides are brown. Remove from the pan and keep moist in a folded dish towel. Repeat with the remaining batter.

5 Arrange the blinis on a serving plate. Top half with soured cream and chopped dill. Spoon 5 ml/1 tsp lumpfish roe on top.

6 Mix the mackerel, butter and lemon rind together and use to top the remaining blinis. Garnish with shredded lemon rind. Serve with lemon wedges.

Porcini Mushroom Pancakes with Chive Butter

Pancakes are an ideal base for subtly flavoured wild mushrooms. Here, porcini mushrooms are contrasted with the fresh flavour of chives. Chanterelle or oyster mushrooms would also work well in this recipe.

Makes 12

INGREDIENTS
50 g/2 oz/4 tbsp unsalted butter
250 g/9 oz porcini mushrooms, chopped
50 g/2 oz porcini mushrooms, sliced
175 g/6 oz/1½ cups self-raising (self-rising)
    flour
2 eggs
200 ml/7 fl oz/scant 1 cup milk
salt and ground white pepper

FOR THE CHIVE BUTTER
15 g/½ oz/scant 1 cup fresh finely
    snipped chives
5 ml/1 tsp lemon juice
115 g/4 oz/½ cup unsalted
    butter, softened

1 First make the chive butter. Stir the snipped chives and lemon juice into the butter. Turn out on to a 25 cm/ 10 in square of greaseproof paper and form into a sausage. Roll up, twist both ends of the paper and chill for about an hour, until it is firm.

2 Melt half the butter in a large pan, add the chopped mushrooms and fry over a moderate heat, allowing the mushrooms to soften and the moisture to evaporate. Spread on to a tray and cool. Cook the sliced mushrooms in a knob of butter and set aside.

3 To make the batter, sift the flour into a bowl and add salt and pepper. Beat the eggs into the milk and add to the flour, stirring to make a thick batter. Add the chopped mushrooms.

4 Heat the remaining butter in a frying pan, arrange five slices of mushrooms at a time in the base, then spoon the batter into 5 cm/2 in circles over each mushroom. When bubbles appear on the surface, turn the pancakes over and cook for 10–15 seconds. Make 12 pancakes in this way. Serve warm with slices of chive butter.

Avocado Cream Blinis

These pancakes are stunning served with a small glass of chilled vodka.

Serves 4

INGREDIENTS
5 ml/1 tsp easy-blend (rapid-rise) dry yeast
250 ml/8 fl oz/1 cup milk, warmed
40 g/1½ oz/⅓ cup buckwheat flour
40 g/1½ oz/⅓ cup plain (all-purpose) flour
10 ml/2 tsp caster (superfine) sugar
pinch of salt
1 egg, separated
vegetable oil, for frying
1 large avocado
75 g/3 oz/⅓ cup fromage blanc
juice of 1 lime
225 g/8 oz beetroot (beet)
45 ml/3 tbsp lime juice
salad leaves, snipped chives and cracked
    black peppercorns, to garnish

1 Mix the yeast and milk, then
mix with the flours, sugar, salt and
egg yolk.

2 Cover with a cloth and leave to
prove for about 40 minutes. Whisk the
egg white until stiff but not dry and
fold into the blini mixture.

3 Heat a little oil in a non-stick pan
and add a ladleful of batter to make
a 10 cm/4 in pancake. Cook for
2–3 minutes on each side. Repeat
with the remaining batter mixture
to make eight blinis.

4 Cut the avocado in half and remove
the stone. Peel and place the flesh in a
blender with the fromage blanc and
lime juice. Blend until smooth.

5 Peel the beetroot and finely shred.
Mix with the lime juice. To serve, top
each blini with a spoonful of avocado
cream. Serve with the beetroot. Garnish
with salad, chives and peppercorns.

Corn Blinis

These blinis are perfect to prepare ahead and take on a summer picnic.

Serves 6–8

INGREDIENTS
75 g/3 oz/⅔ cup plain (all-purpose) flour
75 g/3 oz/⅔ cup wholemeal (whole-wheat)
   flour
250 ml/8 fl oz/1 cup buttermilk
4 small eggs, beaten
2.5 ml/½ tsp salt
25 g/1 oz/2 tbsp butter, melted
pinch of bicarbonate of soda (baking soda)
15 ml/1 tbsp hot water
200 g/7 oz can corn kernels, drained
vegetable oil, for brushing
sliced radishes and fresh dill sprigs,
   to garnish

FOR THE DILL SAUCE
200 g/7 oz/scant 1 cup crème fraîche
30 ml/2 tbsp chopped fresh dill
30 ml/2 tbsp chopped fresh chives
salt and ground black pepper

1 Mix the two flours and buttermilk together until completely smooth. Cover and chill for about 8 hours.

2 Beat in the eggs, salt and butter. Mix the bicarbonate of soda with the hot water and add this with the sweetcorn kernels.

3 Heat a griddle or heavy-based frying pan. Brush with a little oil and drop spoonfuls of the batter on to it.

4 Cook until holes appear on the top. Using a palette knife, flip the blinis over and cook briefly. Stack under a clean dish towel while you make the rest.

5 To make the sauce, blend the crème fraîche with the herbs and seasoning. Serve the blinis with the sauce, garnished with radishes and dill sprigs.

Buckwheat Blinis with Mushroom Caviar

The term caviar is given to fine vegetable mixtures as well as fish roe.

Serves 4

INGREDIENTS
115 g/4 oz/1 cup strong white bread flour
50 g/2 oz/½ cup buckwheat flour
2.5 ml/½ tsp salt
300 ml/½ pint/1¼ cups milk
5 ml/1 tsp dried yeast
2 eggs, separated
vegetable oil, for brushing
200 ml/7 fl oz/scant 1 cup soured cream or
   crème fraîche

FOR THE CAVIAR
350 g/12 oz mixed assorted wild mushrooms
5 ml/1 tsp celery salt
30 ml/2 tbsp walnut oil
15 ml/1 tbsp lemon juice
45 ml/3 tbsp chopped fresh parsley
ground black pepper

1 To make the caviar, trim and chop the mushrooms, then place them in a glass bowl, toss with the celery salt and cover with a weighted plate.

2 Leave the mushrooms for 2 hours until the juices have run out. Rinse the mushrooms thoroughly to remove the salt, drain and press out as much liquid as you can with the back of a spoon. Return them to the bowl and toss with walnut oil, lemon juice, parsley and pepper. Chill until ready to serve.

3 Sift the two flours together with the salt into a large mixing bowl. Warm the milk to blood temperature. Add the yeast, stirring until dissolved, then pour into the flour. Add the egg yolks and stir to make a smooth batter. Cover with a damp cloth and leave in a warm place to rise.

4 Whisk the egg whites in a clean bowl until stiff, then fold into the blini batter.

COOK'S TIP: For the caviar use a mixture of light and dark mushrooms.

5 Heat a heavy-based pan or griddle. Brush with oil, then drop spoonfuls of the batter on to the surface. When bubbles rise to the surface, turn them over and cook briefly on the other side. To serve, top each blini with the mushroom caviar, spoon on the soured cream or crème fraîche, and serve.

Seafood Crêpes

Fresh and smoked haddock combined have a wonderful flavour.

Serves 4–6

INGREDIENTS
1 quantity Basic Crêpe Batter (*see page* 9)
butter, for greasing and brushing
50–75 g/2–3 oz Gruyère cheese, grated
salad leaves, to serve

FOR THE FILLING
225 g/8 oz smoked haddock fillet
225 g/8 oz fresh haddock fillet
300 ml/½ pint/1¼ cups milk
150 ml/¼ pint/⅔ cup single (light) cream
40 g/1½ oz/3 tbsp unsalted butter
40 g/1½ oz/⅓ cup plain (all-purpose)
    flour
freshly grated nutmeg
2 hard-boiled eggs, shelled
    and chopped
salt and ground black pepper

2 Put the haddock fillets in a large pan. Add the milk and poach for 6–8 minutes, until just tender. Lift out the fish using a slotted spoon and, when cool enough to handle, remove the skin and any bones. Reserve the milk.

3 Measure the single cream into a jug, then strain enough of the reserved milk into the jug to make the quantity up to 450 ml/¾ pint/scant 2 cups.

4 Melt the butter in a pan, stir in the flour and cook gently for 1 minute. Gradually mix in the milk mixture, stirring constantly to make a smooth sauce. Cook for 2–3 minutes, until thickened. Season with salt, pepper and nutmeg. Roughly flake the haddock and fold into the sauce with the eggs. Leave to cool.

1 Cook 12 crêpes, using all the batter. As you make them, stack them, interleaved with greaseproof paper, on a plate set over a pan of simmering water to keep them warm while you cook the remainder.

5 Preheat the oven to 180°C/350°F/Gas 4. Divide the filling among the crêpes. Fold the sides of each crêpe into the centre, then roll them up to enclose the filling completely.

6 Butter four or six individual ovenproof dishes and arrange two to three filled crêpes in each, or butter one large dish for all the crêpes. Brush with melted butter and bake for 15 minutes. Sprinkle over the Gruyère and cook for a further 5 minutes, until warmed through. Serve hot with a few salad leaves.

VARIATION: To ring the changes, add cooked, peeled prawns (shrimp), smoked mussels or cooked fresh, shelled mussels to the filling, instead of the chopped hard-boiled eggs.

Chicken & Vegetable Crêpes

Tasting every bit as good as they look, these flavour-packed crêpes are perfect for an informal supper party.

Serves 8

INGREDIENTS
1½ x quantity Basic Crêpe Batter (*see page* 9)
melted butter, for brushing
fresh sage sprigs, to garnish

FOR THE FILLING
30 ml/2 tbsp vegetable oil
3 boneless, skinless chicken breasts, cut into
    fine strips
30 ml/2 tbsp chopped fresh sage
2 leeks, thinly sliced
60 ml/4 tbsp flaked almonds
2 courgettes (zucchini), halved lengthways
    and sliced
30 ml/2 tbsp plain (all-purpose) flour
60 ml/4 tbsp dry sherry
250 ml/8 fl oz/1 cup chicken stock
salt and ground black pepper

1 To make the filling, heat the oil in a flameproof casserole or heavy-based saucepan. Add the chicken, season to taste with salt and pepper and fry over a medium heat, stirring frequently, for 5 minutes, until browned all over.

2 Lower the heat. Add the sage, leeks and almonds and cook, stirring frequently until the leeks are softened.

3 Stir in the courgettes and cook for about 2 minutes. Stir in the flour and cook, stirring constantly for 1 minute.

4 Gradually stir in the sherry and stock and bring to the boil, stirring constantly. Lower the heat and simmer for 10 minutes.

5 Meanwhile, cook 16 crêpes, using all the batter. As you cook them, stack them, interleaved with greaseproof paper, on a plate set over a pan of simmering water to keep warm.

6 When the filling is cooked, taste and adjust the seasoning, if necessary. Divide the filling between the crêpes and fold over. Arrange on individual serving plates, garnish each with a sprig of sage and serve immediately.

COOK'S TIP: An easy and fun way of entertaining is to serve the crêpes and filling separately and let the diners help themselves and fold or roll their own crêpes. For a large party, you could offer several different fillings.

Chicken & Mushroom Crêpes

These crêpes make a very quick and tasty lunch or supper dish.

Serves 4

INGREDIENTS

25 g/1 oz/2 tbsp unsalted butter
1 small onion, finely chopped
50 g/2 oz/scant 1 cup mushrooms,
   finely chopped
30 ml/2 tbsp plain (all-purpose) flour
150 ml/¼ pint/⅔ cup chicken stock or milk
225 g/8 oz cooked chicken, diced
15 ml/1 tbsp fresh parsley, chopped
1 quantity Basic Crêpe Batter (*see page* 9)
vegetable oil, for brushing
30 ml/2 tbsp grated cheese
salt and ground black pepper
watercress, to garnish

1 Melt the butter in a saucepan, add
the onion and cook for 5 minutes,
until softened. Add the mushrooms,
cover and cook for 3–4 minutes.

2 Stir in the flour and cook, stirring
constantly, for 1 minute. Gradually stir
in the stock or milk. Bring to the boil,
stirring constantly, and simmer for
2 minutes. Season, then add the chicken
and parsley. Heat through very gently.

3 Cook eight small or four large
crêpes, using all the batter. Stack them,
interleaved with greaseproof paper, on
a plate set over a pan of simmering
water to keep warm. Preheat the grill
(broiler) and brush an ovenproof dish
with oil.

4 Divide the filling equally among
the crêpes, roll them up and arrange
them in the dish. Brush with a little
oil, sprinkle with cheese and grill
(broil) until melted. Serve hot,
garnished with watercress.

Turkey Crêpe Parcels

Serves 4

INGREDIENTS
30 ml/2 tbsp vegetable oil
450 g/1 lb/4 cups minced (ground) turkey
30 ml/2 tbsp chopped fresh chives
2 green eating apples, cored and diced
25 g/1 oz/¼ cup plain (all-purpose) flour
175 ml/6 fl oz/¾ cup chicken stock
1½ quantity Basic Crêpe Batter (*see page* 9)
vegetable oil, for brushing
60 ml/4 tbsp cranberry sauce
60 ml/4 tbsp chicken stock
15 ml/1 tbsp clear honey
15 g/½ oz/1 tbsp cornflour (cornstarch)
salt and ground black pepper
mangetouts (snowpeas), to serve

1 For the filling, heat the oil in a frying pan. Add the turkey and fry, stirring frequently, for 5 minutes.

2 Add the chives and apples and stir in the flour. Cook, stirring constantly, for 1 minute, then gradually stir in the stock and bring to the boil, stirring constantly. Season to taste and simmer for 20 minutes.

3 Meanwhile, cook 4 large crêpes. Stack them, interleaved with greaseproof paper, on a plate set over a pan of simmering water to keep warm.

4 For the sauce, put the cranberry sauce, stock and honey into a pan. Heat gently, until melted. Blend the cornflour with 1 tbsp water, stir it in and boil, stirring until clear.

5 Spoon the filling into the centre of each crêpe and gather them over around it. Serve with the sauce and mangetouts.

Feta & Spinach Crêpes

A classic combination, cheese and spinach make a melt-in-the-mouth filling for these extra-light crêpes.

Serves 4–6

INGREDIENTS
4 eggs, beaten
40 g/1½ oz/3 tbsp butter, melted
250 ml/8 fl oz/1 cup single (single) cream
250 ml/8 fl oz/1 cup soda water
175 g/6 oz/1½ cups plain (all-purpose) flour, sifted
pinch of salt
vegetable oil, for brushing and frying
1 egg white, lightly beaten
shavings of Parmesan, to garnish

FOR THE FILLING
350 g/12 oz feta cheese, crumbled
50 g/2 oz/⅔ cup freshly grated
   Parmesan cheese
40 g/1½ oz/3 tbsp butter, melted
1 garlic clove, crushed
450 g/1 lb frozen spinach, thawed

1 Process the eggs, butter, cream and soda water in a food processor or blender. With the motor running, add the flour and salt until the batter mixture is smooth. Cover and leave to stand for 15 minutes to rest.

2 Lightly brush a 13–15 cm/5–6 in non-stick frying pan with oil, and place over a medium heat. When hot, pour in 45–60 ml/3–4 tbsp of the batter, tilting the pan to spread the mixture thinly.

3 Cook for about 1½–2 minutes, until the underside of the crêpe is pale golden brown, then flip over and cook on the other side. Repeat the process until all the batter has been used, stacking the crêpes, interleaved with greaseproof paper, on a warm plate.

4 For the filling, mix together the feta, Parmesan, butter and garlic. Squeeze the spinach as dry as possible, then stir in.

5 Place 30–45 ml/2–3 tbsp of the filling mixture on to the centre of each crêpe. Brush a little egg white around the outer edges of the pancakes to moisten, and then fold them over. Press the edges down well to seal.

6 Fry the pancakes in a little oil on both sides, turning gently, until they are golden brown and the filling is hot. Serve immediately, garnished with Parmesan shavings.

Artichoke & Leek Crêpes

Serve crêpes filled with a mouth-watering soufflé mixture of Jerusalem artichokes and leek for a special main course.

Serves 4

INGREDIENTS
¾ quantity Basic Crêpe Batter (*see page* 9)
vegetable oil, for brushing

FOR THE SOUFFLE FILLING
450 g/1 lb Jerusalem artichokes,
   peeled and diced
1 large leek, thinly sliced
50 g/2 oz/4 tbsp unsalted butter
30 ml/2 tbsp self-raising (self-rising)
   flour
30 ml/2 tbsp single (light) cream
75 g/3 oz mature Cheddar cheese, grated
30 ml/2 tbsp chopped fresh parsley
fresh nutmeg, grated
2 eggs, separated
salt and ground black pepper
flat leaf parsley, to garnish

1 Cook eight crêpes, using all the batter. Stack them, interleaved with greaseproof paper, on a plate set over a pan of simmering water.

2 Cook the artichokes and leek with the butter in a covered saucepan on a low heat for about 12 minutes, until very soft. Mash with the back of a wooden spoon. Season to taste. Stir the flour into the vegetables and cook for 1 minute.

3 Off the heat, beat in the cream, cheese, parsley and nutmeg to taste. Cool, then add the egg yolks.

4 Whisk the egg whites until they form soft peaks and fold them into the leek and artichoke mixture.

5 Lightly grease a small ovenproof dish and preheat the oven to 190°C/ 375°F/Gas 5. Fold each crêpe in four, hold the top open and spoon the mixture into the centre. Arrange in the prepared dish with the filling uppermost. Bake for 15 minutes until risen and golden. Serve garnished with parsley.

Roast Asparagus Crêpes

For a really splendid starter, try this simple recipe. Make six large or twelve cocktail-size pancakes.

Serves 6

INGREDIENTS
½ quantity Basic Crêpe Batter (*see page* 9)
vegetable oil, for brushing
90–120 ml/6–8 tbsp olive oil
450 g/1 lb fresh asparagus
175 g/6 oz/¾ cup mascarpone cheese
60 ml/4 tbsp single (light) cream
25 g/1 oz freshly grated
    Parmesan cheese
sea salt

3 Trim the asparagus by placing on a board and cutting off the bases. Using a small, sharp knife, peel away the woody ends, if necessary.

4 Arrange the asparagus in a single layer in the dish, trickle over the remaining olive oil, rolling the asparagus to coat thoroughly. Sprinkle with a little salt and then roast in the oven for about 8–12 minutes, until tender (the cooking time depends on the stem thickness).

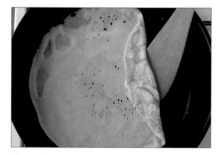

1 Cook six large or 12 small crêpes, using all the batter. Stack them, interleaved with greaseproof paper, on a plate set over a pan of simmering water to keep warm.

2 Preheat the oven to 180°C/350°F/ Gas 4 and lightly grease a large, shallow ovenproof dish or roasting tin with some of the olive oil.

5 Blend the mascarpone with the cream and Parmesan and spread a generous tablespoonful over each of the crêpes, leaving a little extra for the topping. Preheat the grill.

COOK'S TIP: Crêpe batter should always be smooth; strain it if it is lumpy.

6 Divide the roasted asparagus spears among the crêpes, roll up and arrange in a single layer in an ovenproof dish. Spoon over the remaining cheese mixture and place under a moderate grill (broiler) for 4–5 minutes, until heated through and golden brown. Serve at once.

Spinach & Chickpea Crêpes

In this Moroccan-style dish, spinach and courgettes are combined with chickpeas and wrapped in light crêpes.

Serves 4

INGREDIENTS
butter or vegetable oil, for brushing
¾ quantity Basic Crêpe Batter (*see page* 9)

FOR THE FILLING
15 ml/1 tbsp olive oil
1 large onion, chopped
250 g/9 oz fresh spinach
400 g/14 oz can chickpeas, drained
2 courgettes (zucchini), grated
30 ml/2 tbsp chopped fresh coriander
   (cilantro)
2 eggs, beaten
salt and ground black pepper
fresh coriander (cilantro) leaves, to garnish

FOR THE SAUCE
25 g/1 oz/2 tbsp unsalted butter
30 ml/2 tbsp plain (all-purpose) flour
about 300 ml/½ pint/1¼ cups milk

1 On a lightly oiled griddle, cook eight large crêpes on one side only, using all the batter. Set aside.

2 Preheat the oven to 180°C/350°F/ Gas 4. To make the filling, heat the oil in a small frying pan and fry the onion, stirring occasionally, for 4–5 minutes, until soft. Wash the spinach, place in a pan with only the water that clings to the leaves and cook until wilted, shaking the pan occasionally. Chop the spinach roughly.

3 Skin the chickpeas: place them in a bowl of cold water and rub them until the skins float to the surface. Mash the skinned chickpeas roughly with a fork. Add the onion, courgettes, spinach and coriander. Stir in the beaten eggs, season and mix well.

4 Place the crêpes, cooked side up, on a work surface and place large spoonfuls of the filling down the centre. Fold one half of each crêpe over the filling and roll up. Place in a large, buttered ovenproof dish and bake, covered with foil, for about 15 minutes.

5 Meanwhile, melt the butter for the sauce in a small saucepan, stir in the flour and cook, stirring constantly, for 1 minute. Gradually stir in the milk to make a smooth sauce. Season with salt and pepper and pour over the crêpes. Serve the crêpes piping hot, garnished with coriander leaves.

COOK'S TIP: If you prefer, dried chickpeas can be used. Soak 115 g/ 4 oz dried chickpeas overnight in water. Drain, rinse and drain again. Cover with fresh water, boil for 10 minutes and simmer for 1½ hours until tender.

Baked Herb Crêpes

These delicious crêpes make a striking main course at a dinner party.

Serves 4

INGREDIENTS
25 g/1 oz chopped fresh herbs, such as
    parsley, thyme and chervil
15 ml/1 tbsp sunflower oil, plus extra
    for brushing
120 ml/4 fl oz/½ cup milk
3 eggs
25 g/1 oz/¼ cup plain (all-purpose) flour
30 ml/2 tbsp olive oil
1 small onion, chopped
2 garlic cloves, crushed
15 ml/1 tbsp grated fresh ginger root
400 g/14 oz can chopped tomatoes
salt and ground black pepper
salad leaves, to serve

FOR THE FILLING
450 g/1 lb fresh spinach
175 g/6 oz/¾ cup ricotta cheese
25 g/1 oz/2 tbsp pine nuts, toasted
5 halves sun-dried tomatoes in olive oil,
    drained and chopped
30 ml/2 tbsp shredded fresh basil
grated nutmeg
4 egg whites

1 To make the crêpes, place the fresh
herbs and oil in a blender and process
until smooth, pushing down any
whole pieces with a spatula. Add the
milk, eggs, flour and a pinch of salt
and process again until smooth and
pale green in colour. Leave to rest for
30 minutes.

2 Heat a small non-stick crêpe or
frying pan and brush with oil. Add a
ladleful of the batter and swirl
around to cover the base. Cook for
1–2 minutes, turn over and cook the
other side. Repeat with the remaining
batter to make eight crêpes.

3 To make the sauce, heat the oil in a
small pan. Add the onion, garlic and
ginger and cook gently for 5 minutes,
until softened. Add the tomatoes and
cook for a further 10–15 minutes,
until the mixture thickens. Purée, sieve
and set aside.

4 To make the filling, wash the
spinach and place in a large pan with
only the water that clings to the leaves.
Cover and cook, stirring once, until
just wilted. Remove from the heat and
refresh in cold water. Place in a sieve
or colander, squeeze out the excess
water and chop finely. Mix the spinach
with the ricotta, pine nuts, sun-dried
tomatoes and basil. Season with
nutmeg, salt and pepper.

5 Preheat the oven to 190°C/375°F/ Gas 5. Whisk the egg whites until stiff but not dry. Fold one-third into the spinach and ricotta to lighten the mixture, then gently fold in the rest.

6 Taking one crêpe at a time, place on a lightly oiled baking sheet. Place a large spoonful of filling on each one and fold into quarters. Repeat until all the filling and crêpes are used up. Bake for 10–15 minutes, or until set. Reheat the tomato sauce, and serve with the crêpes and crisp salad leaves.

Honeycomb Pancakes

Arrange the cooked pancakes in a honeycomb pattern, before serving
with butter, warm honey, cinnamon and perhaps a few dates.

Serves 3–4

INGREDIENTS
175 g/6 oz/1½ cups self-raising (self-rising)
    flour
10 ml/2 tsp baking powder
30 ml/2 tbsp caster (superfine) sugar
1 egg
175 ml/6 fl oz/¾ cup semi-skimmed (low-
    fat) milk
15 ml/1 tbsp rose flower water
15 ml/1 tbsp melted butter
vegetable oil, for brushing

1 Mix together the flour, baking
powder and sugar. Add the egg and
milk and blend. Stir in the rose water
and then beat in the melted butter.

2 Heat a frying pan and brush the
surface with a little oil. Pour in a small
ladleful of batter, smoothing with the
back of the spoon to make a round
about 10 cm/4 in across. Cook for a
few minutes, until bubbles appear on
the surface, then place on a large plate.

3 Cook the remaining pancakes in
the same way and place them on the
plate in overlapping circles to make a
honeycomb pattern. Serve warm.

VARIATION: Replace the rose
water with orange flower water for
an equally delicious taste.

Oaty Pancakes with Caramel Bananas

Serves 4

INGREDIENTS
75 g/3 oz/⅔ cup plain (all-purpose) flour
50 g/2 oz/½ cup wholemeal (whole-wheat)
    flour
50 g/2 oz/½ cup porridge oats
5 ml/1 tsp baking powder
25 g/1 oz/2 tbsp caster (superfine) sugar
1 egg
15 ml/1 tbsp sunflower oil, plus extra
    for brushing
250 ml/8 fl oz/1 cup milk
salt
50 g/2 oz/4 tbsp unsalted butter
15 ml/1 tbsp maple syrup
3 bananas, halved and quartered lengthways
25 g/1 oz/¼ cup pecan nuts

1 To make the pancakes, mix together the flours, oats, baking powder, sugar and a pinch of salt in a bowl.

2 Make a well in the centre and add the egg, oil and a quarter of the milk. Mix well, then gradually add the rest of the milk to make a thick batter. Leave to rest for 20 minutes in the fridge.

3 Heat a large, heavy-based, lightly oiled frying pan. Using about 30 ml/ 2 tbsp of batter for each pancake, cook two to three pancakes at a time. Cook for 3 minutes on each side, or until golden. Keep warm while you cook the remaining pancakes.

4 Wipe out the frying pan and melt the butter. Add the maple syrup and stir well. Add the bananas and pecan nuts. Cook, turning once, for about 4 minutes, or until the bananas have softened and the sauce has just caramelized. Serve the pancakes with the bananas and nuts.

Blueberry Pancakes

These are like the usual thick American-style breakfast pancakes – though they can, of course, be eaten at any time of the day.

Serves 2

INGREDIENTS
115 g/4 oz/1 cup self-raising (self-rising) flour
pinch of salt
45–60 ml/3–4 tbsp caster (superfine) sugar
2 eggs
120 ml/4 fl oz/½ cup milk
15–30 ml/1–2 tbsp vegetable oil
115 g/4 oz/1 cup fresh or frozen blueberries
maple syrup, to serve

1 Sift the flour into a bowl with the salt and sugar. Beat together the eggs thoroughly. Make a well in the centre and stir in the eggs. Gradually blend in a little of the milk to make a smooth batter. Then whisk in the rest of the milk and whisk for 1–2 minutes. Allow to rest for 20–30 minutes.

2 Heat a few drops of oil in a pancake pan or heavy-based frying pan until just hazy. Pour in about 30 ml/ 2 tbsp of the batter and swirl it around until it makes an even shape.

3 Cook for 2–3 minutes and when almost set on top, sprinkle over 15–30 ml/1–2 tbsp blueberries. As soon as the base is loose and golden brown, turn the pancake over. Cook on the second side for about 1 minute, until golden and crisp. Slide the pancake on to a plate and serve drizzled with maple syrup. Continue with the rest of the batter.

VARIATION: Try blackberries instead of the blueberries.

Chocolate Chip Banana Pancakes

These delicious pancakes, served as a dessert, are sure to be popular.

Serves 3–4

INGREDIENTS
2 ripe bananas
200 ml/7 fl oz/scant 1 cup milk
2 eggs
150 g/5 oz/1¼ cups self-raising (self-rising) flour
25 g/1 oz/¼ cup ground almonds
15 ml/1 tbsp caster (superfine) sugar
pinch of salt
25 g/1 oz plain chocolate chips
25 g/1 oz/2 tbsp butter

FOR THE TOPPING
150 ml/¼ pint/⅔ cup double (heavy) cream
15 ml/1 tbsp icing sugar
50 g/2 oz/½ cup toasted flaked (sliced) almonds, to decorate

1 In a bowl, mash the bananas with a fork, combine with half of the milk and beat in the eggs. Sieve in the flour, ground almonds, sugar and salt. Make a well in the centre and pour in the remaining milk. Add the chocolate chips and stir to produce a thick batter.

2 Heat a knob of butter in a non-stick frying pan. Spoon the batter into heaps, allowing room for them to spread. When bubbles emerge, turn the pancakes over and cook briefly on the other side.

3 Loosely whip the cream with the icing sugar to sweeten it slightly. Spoon the cream on to the pancakes and decorate with flaked almonds.

Chocolate & Orange Scotch Pancakes

Baby chocolatey pancakes with a rich, creamy orange liqueur sauce.

Serves 4

INGREDIENTS
115 g/4 oz/1 cup self-raising (self-rising) flour
30 ml/2 tbsp cocoa powder
2 eggs
50 g/2 oz plain chocolate, chopped into
    small pieces
200 ml/7 fl oz/scant 1 cup milk
finely grated rind of 1 orange
30 ml/2 tbsp orange juice
vegetable oil, for brushing
chocolate curls, to decorate

FOR THE SAUCE
2 large oranges
25 g/1 oz/2 tbsp unsalted butter
45 ml/3 tbsp light muscovado (brown) sugar
250 ml/8 fl oz/1 cup crème fraîche
30 ml/2 tbsp Grand Marnier or Cointreau

1 Sift the flour and cocoa into a bowl and make a well in the centre. Add the eggs and beat well, gradually incorporating the dry ingredients.

2 Mix the chocolate and milk in a saucepan. Heat gently until the chocolate has melted, then beat into the mixture until smooth and bubbly. Stir in the orange rind and juice to make a batter.

3 Heat a large, heavy-based frying pan or griddle. Brush with a little oil. Drop large spoonfuls of batter on to the hot surface, leaving room for spreading.

4 Cook over a moderate heat. When the pancakes are lightly browned underneath and bubbly on top, flip over to cook the other side. Slide on to a plate and keep hot, then make more in the same way.

5 Make the sauce. Grate the rind of one orange into a bowl and set aside. Peel both oranges, taking care to remove all the pith, then slice the flesh fairly thinly into rounds.

6 Heat the butter and sugar in a wide, shallow pan over a low heat, stirring until the sugar dissolves. Stir in the crème fraîche and heat gently.

7 Add the chocolate pancakes and orange slices to the sauce, heat gently for 1–2 minutes, then spoon over the liqueur. Sprinkle with the reserved orange rind. Scatter over the chocolate curls and serve the pancakes at once, straight from the pan.

45

Rum & Banana Waffles

To save time, these scrumptious dessert waffles can be made in advance, wrapped tightly, frozen, and then warmed through in the oven just before serving. The topping takes only a few minutes to prepare and cook.

Serves 4

INGREDIENTS

225 g/8 oz/2 cups plain (all-purpose) flour
10 ml/2 tsp baking powder
5 ml/1 tsp bicarbonate of soda (baking soda)
15 ml/1 tbsp caster (superfine) sugar
2 eggs
50 g/2 oz/4 tbsp butter, melted
175 ml/6 fl oz/¾ cup milk, plus extra
   if needed
300 ml/½ pint/1¼ cups buttermilk
5 ml/1 tsp pure vanilla extract
single (light) cream, to serve

FOR THE BANANAS

6 bananas, thickly sliced
115 g/4 oz/1 cup pecan nuts,
   broken into pieces
50 g/2 oz/¼ cup demerara (raw) sugar
75 ml/5 tbsp maple syrup
45 ml/3 tbsp dark rum

1 Sift the dry ingredients into a large mixing bowl. Make a well in the centre. Add the eggs, melted butter and milk. Whisk together, gradually incorporating the flour mixture, until the batter is smooth.

2 Add the buttermilk and vanilla to the batter and whisk well. Cover and leave to stand for 30 minutes. Preheat the oven to 150°C/300°F/Gas 2.

3 Heat a hand-held waffle iron over the heat. Stir the batter and add more milk if required (the consistency should be quite thick). Open the waffle iron and pour some batter over two-thirds of the surface. Close it and wipe off any excess batter.

4 Cook for 3–4 minutes, carefully turning the waffle iron over once during cooking. If using an electric waffle maker, follow the manufacturer's instructions for cooking.

5 When the batter stops steaming, open the iron and lift out the waffle with a fork. Put it on a heatproof plate and keep it hot in the oven. Repeat, to make eight waffles in all. Preheat the grill (broiler).

COOK'S TIP: If you don't own a waffle iron, use the mixture to make small pancakes.

6 To cook the bananas, spread them out on a large, shallow baking tin and top with the broken pecan nuts. Scatter over the demerara sugar. Mix the maple syrup and rum together and spoon over. Grill (broil) for 3–4 minutes or until the sugar begins to bubble. Serve on top of the waffles with cream.

Blueberry & Orange Crêpe Baskets

Impress your guests with these pretty, fruit-filled crêpes. When blueberries are out of season, replace them with other soft fruit, such as raspberries.

Serves 6–8

INGREDIENTS
150 g/5 oz/1¼ cups plain (all-purpose) flour
2 egg whites
200 ml/7 fl oz/scant 1 cup milk
150 ml/¼ pint/⅔ cup orange juice
vegetable oil, for brushing
salt
natural (plain) yogurt or crème fraîche,
   to serve

FOR THE FILLING
4 medium-size oranges
225 g/8 oz/2 cups blueberries

1 Preheat the oven to 200°C/400°F/ Gas 6. To make the crêpes, sift the flour and a pinch of salt into a bowl. Make a well in the centre and add the egg whites, milk and orange juice. Whisk hard, until all the liquid has been incorporated and the batter is smooth and bubbly.

2 Brush a heavy-based or non-stick crêpe pan with vegetable oil and heat it until it is very hot. Pour in just enough batter to cover the base of the pan, lifting and swirling it to cover the pan evenly.

3 Cook until the crêpe has set and is golden, then turn it to cook the other side. Remove to a sheet of absorbent kitchen paper and cook the remaining batter to make six to eight crêpes.

4 Place six to eight small ovenproof bowls or moulds on a baking sheet and arrange the crêpes over these. Bake them in the oven for about 10 minutes, until they are crisp and set into shape. Carefully lift the "baskets" off the moulds.

5 Pare a thin piece of orange rind from one orange and cut it in fine strips. Blanch the strips in boiling water for 30 seconds, rinse in cold water and set aside. Cut all the peel and white pith from all the oranges.

COOK'S TIP: Don't fill the crêpe baskets until you're ready to serve.

6 Divide the oranges into segments, catching the juice in a bowl. Combine the orange segments and the reserved juice with the blueberries and warm them gently. Spoon the fruit into the baskets and scatter the shreds of rind over the top. Serve with yogurt or crème fraîche.

49

Apple & Cinnamon Buckwheat Crêpes

Spiced pan-fried apple slices create a scrumptious topping for these buckwheat crêpes. Pears also taste great served this way.

Serves 4

INGREDIENTS
3 cooking apples, peeled, cored and sliced
50 g/2 oz/¼ cup caster (superfine) sugar
50 g/2 oz/4 tbsp unsalted butter
30–45 ml/2–3 tbsp brandy
5–10 ml/1–2 tsp ground cinnamon
fresh mint sprigs, to garnish
crème fraîche and cinnamon, to serve

FOR THE CREPES
50 g/2 oz/½ cup buckwheat flour
50 g/2 oz/½ cup rice flour
1 egg
300 ml/½ pint/1¼ cups semi-skimmed
    (low-fat) milk
sunflower oil, for brushing
salt

1 Make the crêpes. Place the flours and a pinch of salt in a bowl and make a well in the centre. Break in the egg and add a little of the milk, beating well. Gradually beat in the remaining milk, drawing the flour in from the sides to make a smooth batter.

2 Brush an 18 cm/7 in non-stick frying pan with oil. Pour in enough batter to coat the base of the pan thinly. Cook until golden brown, then turn and cook on the other side.

3 Transfer the cooked crêpe to a warmed plate and keep hot. Repeat with the remaining batter to make eight crêpes in all. Stack the crêpes, interleaved with greaseproof paper, on the plate set over a pan of simmering water to keep warm.

4 Toss the apple slices in the caster sugar in a mixing bowl.

5 Melt the butter in a large frying pan, add the apple slices and cook over a high heat, stirring frequently, for about 5 minutes, until the apple slices soften slightly and the sugar has caramelized. Remove the pan from the heat and sprinkle the apples with the brandy and cinnamon.

6 Serve the crêpes topped with the apples and some crème fraîche sprinkled with cinnamon, and garnished with mint.

Layered Almond Crêpe Gâteau

Thicker than usual, these crêpes are layered with a creamy almond filling and topped with soured cream to make a tempting dessert.

Serves 6

INGREDIENTS
5 eggs, separated
50 g/2 oz/½ cup caster (superfine) sugar
175 ml/6 fl oz/¾ cup milk
50 g/2 oz/½ cup self-raising (self-rising) flour, sifted
50 g/2 oz/4 tbsp unsalted butter, melted
175 ml/6 fl oz/¾ cup soured cream
sifted icing (confectioners') sugar, for dredging
lemon wedges, to serve

FOR THE FILLING
3 eggs, separated
25 g/1 oz/¼ cup icing (confectioners') sugar, sifted
grated rind of 1 lemon
2.5 ml/½ tsp vanilla sugar
115 g/4 oz/1 cup ground almonds

1 Preheat the oven to 200°C/400°F/ Gas 6. Grease and base-line a deep 20–23 cm/8–9 in springform cake tin (pan). Whisk the egg yolks and caster sugar together until thick and creamy, then whisk in the milk.

2 Whisk the egg whites until stiff, then fold into the batter mixture, alternating with spoonfuls of the flour and half the melted butter.

3 Brush a frying pan with butter as near to the size of your cake tin as possible. Tip one-quarter of the batter into the frying pan. Fry the crêpe on each side until golden brown, then slide it into the prepared cake tin. Use up the batter to make three more crêpes in the same way and set them aside while you make the filling.

4 Whisk the egg yolks in a bowl with the icing sugar until thick and creamy. Stir in the lemon rind and the vanilla sugar. Whisk the egg whites in a separate bowl, then fold them into the egg yolk mixture and add the ground almonds. Mix together well.

5 Spread one-third of the mixture on top of the first crêpe. Cover with the second crêpe, and repeat the layering, finishing with the fourth crêpe.

6 Spread the soured cream over the top and bake for 20–25 minutes, or until the top is pale golden brown. Leave in the tin for 10 minutes before turning out and removing the lining paper. Serve warm, cut into wedges, dusted with icing sugar and accompanied by lemon wedges.

Polish Crêpes

In Poland, traditional crêpes are filled with a cheese and sultana mixture.

Makes 6

INGREDIENTS
115 g/4 oz/1 cup plain (all-purpose) flour
pinch of freshly grated nutmeg, plus extra
for dusting
1 egg, separated
200 ml/7 fl oz/scant 1 cup milk
30 ml/2 tbsp sunflower oil
25 g/1 oz/2 tbsp unsalted butter
salt
lemon slices, to decorate

FOR THE FILLING
225 g/8 oz/1 cup curd cheese
15 ml/1 tbsp caster (superfine) sugar
5 ml/1 tsp vanilla extract
50 g/2 oz/scant ½ cup sultanas (golden
raisins)

1 Sift the flour, nutmeg and a pinch of salt together in a large bowl. Make a well in the centre. Add the egg yolk and half the milk. Beat until smooth, then gradually beat in the remaining milk. Whisk the egg white in a bowl until stiff. Fold into the batter.

2 Heat 5 ml/1 tsp sunflower oil and a little of the butter in an 18 cm/7 in frying pan. Pour in enough of the batter to cover the base. Cook for 2 minutes, until golden brown, then turn over and cook for a further 2 minutes.

3 Make five more crêpes in the same way. Stack the crêpes, interleaved with greaseproof paper, on a plate set over a pan of simmering water.

4 To make the filling, put the curd cheese, sugar and vanilla extract in a bowl and beat together. Mix in the sultanas. Divide among the crêpes, fold them and dust with nutmeg. Serve with lemon slices.

Chocolate Crêpes with Plums & Port

An impressive dinner party dessert that can be prepared in advance.

Serves 5-6

INGREDIENTS
50 g/2 oz plain (semisweet) chocolate,
  chopped into small pieces
200 ml/7 fl oz/scant 1 cup milk
120 ml/4 fl oz/½ cup single (light) cream
30 ml/2 tbsp cocoa powder
115 g/4 oz/1 cup plain (all-purpose) flour
2 eggs
oil, for brushing

FOR THE FILLING
500 g/1¼ lb red or golden plums
50 g/2 oz/¼ cup caster (superfine) sugar
30 ml/2 tbsp water
30 ml/2 tbsp port
150 g/5 oz/¾ cup crème fraîche or
  Greek yogurt (US strained plain)

FOR THE SAUCE
150 g/5 oz plain (semisweet) chocolate,
  chopped into small pieces
175 ml/6 fl oz/¾ cup double (heavy) cream
15 ml/1 tbsp port

1 Make the crêpe batter. Place the chocolate in a saucepan with the milk. Heat gently, stirring occasionally, until the chocolate has melted. Pour into a blender or food processor and add the cream, cocoa, flour and eggs. Process until smooth, then tip into a jug and chill for 30 minutes.

2 Meanwhile, make the filling. Halve and stone the plums. Place them in a saucepan and add the caster sugar and water. Bring to the boil, then lower the heat, cover and simmer for about 10 minutes, or until the plums are tender. Stir in the port, taking care not to break up the plums, then simmer for a further 30 seconds. Remove from the heat and keep warm.

3 Have ready a sheet of non-stick baking paper. Heat a crêpe pan, brush it lightly with a little oil, then pour in just enough batter to cover the base, swirling to coat evenly.

4 Cook until the crêpe has set, then flip it over to cook the other side. Slide the crêpe out on to the sheet of paper, then cook nine to eleven more in the same way. It should not be necessary to add more oil to the pan, but if the crêpes start to stick, add a very light coating.

5 Make the sauce. Combine the chocolate pieces and cream in a saucepan. Heat gently, stirring until smooth. Add the port to the saucepan and heat the mixture gently, stirring, for 1 minute.

6 Divide the plum filling among the crêpes, add a spoon of crème fraîche or Greek-style yogurt to each and roll them up carefully. Serve in individual bowls, with the chocolate sauce spooned over the top of each portion.

Summer Berry Crêpes

The delicate flavour of these fluffy crêpes contrasts beautifully with tangy berry fruits, flambéed in orange liqueur.

Serves 4

INGREDIENTS
115 g/4 oz/1 cup self-raising (self-rising)
  flour
1 large egg
300 ml/½ pint/1¼ cups milk
a few drops of vanilla extract
15 g/½ oz/1 tbsp unsalted butter
15 ml/1 tbsp sunflower oil
icing (confectioners') sugar, for dusting

FOR THE FRUIT
25 g/1 oz/2 tbsp unsalted butter
50 g/2 oz/¼ cup caster (superfine) sugar
juice of 2 oranges
thinly pared rind of ½ orange
350 g/12 oz/3 cups mixed summer berries,
  such as sliced strawberries, raspberries,
  blueberries and redcurrants
45 ml/3 tbsp orange liqueur

1 Preheat the oven to 150°C/300°F/ Gas 2. To make the crêpes, sift the flour into a large bowl and make a well in the centre. Break in the egg and gradually whisk in the milk to make a smooth batter. Stir in the vanilla essence. Set the batter aside for 30 minutes.

COOK'S TIP: For safety, when igniting a mixture for flambéing, use a long taper or long wooden match.

2 Heat the butter and oil together in an 18 cm/7 in non-stick frying pan. Swirl to grease the pan, then pour off the excess. If the batter has been allowed to stand, whisk it thoroughly until smooth. Pour a little of the batter into the pan, swirling to cover the base evenly. Cook until the mixture comes away from the sides and the crêpe is golden underneath.

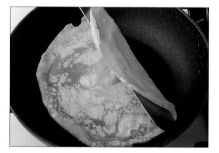

3 Flip over the crêpe with a large palette knife and cook the other side briefly until golden. Slide the crêpe on to a plate. Make seven more crêpes in the same way, greasing the pan with more butter and oil mixture as needed. Stack the crêpes, interleaved with greaseproof paper, on a plate set over a pan of simmering water to keep hot.

4 To prepare the fruit, melt the butter in a heavy-based frying pan, stir in the sugar and cook gently until the mixture is golden brown. Add the orange juice and rind and cook until syrupy.

5 Add the fruits and warm through, then add the liqueur and set it alight. Shake the pan to incorporate the liqueur until the flame dies down.

6 Fold the crêpes into quarters and arrange two on each plate. Spoon over some of the fruit mixture and dust liberally with the icing sugar. Serve any remaining fruit mixture separately.

Banana & Lime Crêpes

These quick and easy, fruit-filled crêpes will soon become a firm favourite.

Serves 4

INGREDIENTS
115 g/4 oz/1 cup plain (all-purpose) flour
1 egg white
250 ml/8 fl oz/1 cup milk
50 ml/2 fl oz/¼ cup cold water
sunflower oil, for brushing
strips of lime rind, to decorate
yogurt or fromage frais, to serve

FOR THE FILLING
4 bananas, sliced
45 ml/3 tbsp maple syrup or golden syrup
30 ml/2 tbsp lime juice

1 Beat together the flour, egg white, milk and water until smooth and bubbly. Chill until needed.

2 Brush a non-stick frying pan with oil, heat it and pour in enough batter just to coat the base. Swirl it around the pan to coat evenly.

3 Cook until golden, then flip over and cook the other side. Transfer to a plate and make seven more crêpes, using all the batter. Stack the crêpes, interleaved with greaseproof paper, on a plate set over a pan of simmering water to keep warm.

4 Place the bananas, syrup and lime juice in a pan and simmer gently for 1 minute. Spoon into the pancakes and fold into quarters. Sprinkle with lime strips and serve hot, with yogurt or fromage frais.

Pineapple Crêpes

Prepare the pineapple in advance for this delicious dessert.

Serves 8

INGREDIENTS
1½ quantity Basic Crêpe Batter (*see page* 9)
vegetable oil, for brushing
natural (plain) yogurt, to serve

FOR THE FILLING
1 fresh, ripe pineapple
120 ml/4 fl oz/½ cup maple syrup

1 First, prepare the filling. Cut the base and leafy top off the pineapple. Cut away the peel and cut away the "eyes". Cut the pineapple into slices and stamp out the hard woody core with a biscuit cutter. Alternatively, cut the fruit in half lengthways and cut out the core in a wedge shape.

2 Cut the pineapple flesh into small pieces. Put the pieces in a bowl and trickle over the maple syrup. Cover and chill in the fridge for 2 hours.

3 Cook 16 crêpes, using all the batter. As you cook them, stack them, interleaved with greaseproof paper, on a plate set over a pan of simmering water to keep warm.

4 Toss the pineapple in the syrup and divide it equally among the crêpes. Fold them over, top with a spoonful of yogurt and serve immediately.

COOK'S TIP: Try to find pure maple syrup for this recipe.

Crêpes Suzette with Cointreau & Cognac

Crêpes filled with Cointreau-flavoured butter and flambéed with cognac may be a classic, but they remain as popular as ever.

Serves 6

INGREDIENTS
½ quantity Basic Crêpe Batter (*see page* 9)
oil, for brushing
juice of 2 oranges
45 ml/3 tbsp cognac
icing (confectioners') sugar, for dusting
strips of thinly pared orange rind, to decorate

FOR THE ORANGE BUTTER
175 g/6 oz/¾ cup unsalted butter
50 g/2 oz/¼ cup granulated (white) sugar
grated rind of 2 oranges
30 ml/2 tbsp Cointreau

1 First, make the orange butter. Cream the butter with the sugar in a bowl. Stir in the orange rind and Cointreau. Set aside.

2 Cook six crêpes, using all the batter. As you cook them, stack them, interleaved with greaseproof paper, on a plate set over a pan of simmering water to keep warm.

VARIATION: Not traditional, but equally delicious, is to use rum in place of the Cointreau and cognac, and add sliced fresh pineapple and a little toasted coconut.

3 Spread the crêpes with half the orange butter and fold into quarters.

4 Heat the remaining orange butter in a frying pan with the orange juice. Add the folded crêpes and turn them to heat them through. Push the crêpes to one side of the pan and pour in the cognac. Heat, then carefully set alight. When the flames die down, spoon the sauce over the crêpes.

5 Serve immediately, dusted with icing sugar and decorated with strips of orange rind.

Index

This edition is published by Lorenz Books,
an imprint of Anness Publishing Ltd,
108 Great Russell Street, London WC1B 3NA info@anness.com

www.lorenzbooks.com; www.annesspublishing.com

© Anness Publishing Limited 2014

If you like the images in this book and would like to investigate
using them for publishing, promotions or advertising, please visit
our website www.practicalpictures.com for more information.

Publisher: Joanna Lorenz
Editor: Valerie Ferguson & Helen Sudell
Designer: Andrew Heath
Production Controller: Pirong Wang

Recipes contributed by: Catherine Atkinson, Alex Barker,
Frances Cleary, Trish Davies, Roz Denny, Christine France,
Shirley Gill, Nicola Graimes, Rebekah Hassan, Christine Ingram,
Judy Jackson, Bridget Jones, Norma MacMillan, Sue Maggs,
Maggie Mayhew, Christine McFadden, Norma Miller,
Annie Nichols, Anne Sheasby, Jenny Stacey, Steven Wheeler.

Photography: William Adams-Lingwood, Karl Adamson,
Steve Baxter, James Duncan, Ian Garlick, Amanda Heywood,
David Jordan, Don Last, Patrick McLeavey, Michael Michaels,
Thomas Odulate.

COOK'S NOTES

Bracketed terms are intended for American readers.

For all recipes, quantities are given in both metric and imperial
measures and, where appropriate, in standard cups and spoons.
Follow one set of measures, but not a mixture, because they are
not interchangeable.

Standard spoon and cup measures are level. 1 tsp = 5ml, 1 tbsp =
15ml, 1 cup = 250ml/8fl oz. Australian standard tablespoons are
20ml. Australian readers should use 3 tsp
in place of 1 tbsp for measuring small quantities.

American pints are 16fl oz/2 cups. American readers should use
20fl oz/2.5 cups in place of 1 pint when measuring liquids.

Electric oven temperatures in this book are for conventional
ovens. When using a fan oven, the temperature will probably
need to be reduced by about 10–20°C/20–40°F. Since ovens
vary, you should check with your manufacturer's instruction
book for guidance.

Medium (US large) eggs are used unless otherwise stated.

PUBLISHER'S NOTE:
Although the advice and information in this book are believed
to be accurate and true at the time of going to press, neither the
authors nor the publisher can accept any legal responsibility or
liability for any errors or omissions that may have been made nor
for any inaccuracies nor for any loss, harm or injury that comes
about from following instructions or advice in this book.